Morning Always Comes

Poems

Richard Sievers

Morning Always Comes
Poems

Copyright © 2011 Richard Sievers

Field of Seven Houses Publishing
Battle Ground, Washington, USA
www. fieldofsevenhouses.com

e-mail:
fieldofsevenhouses@yahoo.com

ISBN: 978-0-9829207-1-8

Library of Congress Control Number: 2011941176

Cover Art and Design by Richard Sievers © 2011

For Heather

Other Book by Richard Sievers:

<u>Earth, My Body</u> published 2010
by Field of Seven Houses Publishing

Background on the Poems:

Included in this volume are early poems I wrote over a five-year period. I made a commitment to write at least one small book of poetry a year and these poems are distilled from this effort. They reflect an emerging sense of wonder found in poetry and love presented here in a timeline of watershed life events. They document the seasons of the heart, living through love, losing many things I once thought were important, death and finding a home once more.

All of the poems have been reworked and re-imagined over the years. Created works are not stagnant objects. They are living beings, viable and dynamic and, like humans, capable of change. Editing these pieces has been a joy and a cathartic experience. Like memory, the past is overlaid with hard-won wisdom. The past is here and now. Somehow, by diving into strong memories, the pain of soul and body can find a greater sense of healing.

All of these pieces were sent in to contests or publishers. All but one were rejected. *Too spiritual. Not a clear story. Too sentimental.* These were the comments I received from the reviewers…when I received anything at all. Perhaps like you, I did not fit in the mold. Most people do not fit in the strictures of what our society prescribes without giving away part of their soul. Several of these poems were included in a subsequent self-published volume, Earth, My Body.

Here they are, novice deficiencies and all. I hope that they are healing for you during transitions of love and loss and rebirth. I hope they inspire you to live beyond perfectionism or capitulation. I hope that you can hear your own stories in these poems. I hope they help you to remain persistent in singing your particular song, whether it is popular or not.

Thanks for reading.

Rick Sievers
October 2011

Morning Always Comes

Table of Contents

The Fallen 2006

The Working of the Winds 2007-2008

Buying the Farm 2009

Season of Crossing

2 0 0 4

Epitaph

~~~

He launched his kayak
into the laughing
storm, toward the dark
island and the song-lit windows of his
home, just out there,
safe on the other shore.

You Came to Me

When the spring rain slanted toward summer,
when the wide green fields became heavy,
when the Beltane fire was smoldering coals,
you came to me.
When the door frame donned morning spider webs,
when the robin's sonnet drifted across the writing desk,
when I woke as a bear from a bone-damp cave,
you came to me.
When you were a ribbon of sun fluttering in the walnut tree,
when you rested in the prayers of our dew-seasoned porch,
when you danced in my hair with the feet of a linen butterfly,
you came to me.
When the face of a yellow rose kissed the window,
when I believed in the devotion of a sparrow feeding her children,
when you fell into the blood of autumn and whispered
Soon, my love, soon…

Cottonwood River

You know the sound:
clapping leaves,
silver on the bottom,
greenback on top,
slapping shore,
waves above,
grass below.
~

The cottonwood casts
her prayers into spring,
white and gold.
You know that smell,
deep sucking mud oozing
around her clawing roots,
the bright and bitter bark
twisting in a pirouette
of sticky rain.

You know the feeling
of sand and stones
passing from hand to hand,
the shudder of wind
upon your skin, the flicker
of sparrow wings in your sunrise.
Lie back, remember
our day of crying on Columbia's shoulder.
You know the place to lie
on the beach of entwining
branches grasping at the sky
and leaves of cotton exploding
into nothing.
~

You trembled there.
Rising spring,
morning sun,
heat spread
thin beneath open arms
of shattered wood.
You know the time
that sieved into foaming currents,
buried deep in pools
covered in tremulous shadows,
where a sweet scent was rising
into ether with webbed prayers
of white and gold.
Dancers were twisting
just above the undertow so long ago.

You remember the cottonwood.

Four Poems on the American War

He died face down
in a muddy bowl
of blood and oil.
He fell out of his shivering
skin, washed away
in a desert storm, shadowed
by the power of air and fire.
Alone.

~

A family of three,
with one on the way,
watches him die on their dinner-
time television.
The perfumed mother chews
on the end of the world.
One by one she watches them,
their faces bent
into the mud. The dead were
turning their backs on hell.
They turned from the eyes
digesting a dinner as cold as the rain,
tasteless as the bones floating
in an earthen bowl of mud and oil.

~

The television channel is changed
with a click of a trigger.
A preacher flashes on the holy network.
He struts in the crystal tower
choir lofts of well-wishers
raising their hands in praise.
He shouts out God's words:
I am the way the truth and the life.
And another son dies with his hands up
in the rapture of heaven's draft.
Eat, for this is my body.
And another shroud of blood
red, bruised blue and white
blanched flesh flies home.
Drink, for this is my blood given to you for the remission of sins.

The family of three,
with one on the way,
stare down into the flickering static.
Love your neighbor as yourself.
The preacher moans.
The little girl pulls out strands of her perfect curls.
If a man strikes you, turn the other cheek.
The father sighs, finished with his greasy soup.

He flicks to another channel with a laugh
track and a pretend family.
He turns his pie-balled stare
toward the window and the rain,
falling down in a drum tap
of soot from another land.
~
He dies face down
in a bowl of blood and grease.
He stares at the final tremble of his
hands moving from storm to storm,
washed in the shadows of air and fire.

Alone

The Poem's Horse

Like Frost's Horse, I step into someone else's woods,
astounded by a moment of luminous snowfall.
I catch the snowflakes in wonder.
They fall upon my shaggy coat,
melting in my breath,
running cold and
fluid upon my lips and throat.

I am the Poem's horse
moving deep into the night,
me with my load,
my master with his whip.
And miles to go,
back to the desk by the sea,
back to carnal city streets,
back to the meadow of dreams.
Carrying the forest within me.
Closing my eyes.
Soon, mountains of lace and
crystal rivers are falling
down into the dark earth.

Second Draft...
Half-Lit at the Brown Lantern Bar

A siren sings just offshore of a weathered seaport street:
Come to the circle, poet.
Come home to our family,
dark and dirty and guilty
of pleasure's song.

Poets can lift whatever
they want and call it
"higher truth," even a parting
glass. The center of the world
is where The Word is raised by bards,
dreaming, half-lit at the Brown Lantern.

A martini, a greyhound, a Guinness, a Bud Light,
a whiskey neat, an empty glass.
So many names swirling
from the smirking lips
of the ghosts circling
this stewing bowl of cigarettes.

"Words are power," an old salt yells.
Another man leans further into his beer.
One holds his pen ready to write,
twirling his wand, longing
to score a forgotten phrase,
maybe even finding a phrase uttered by
angels, above and below
this wave plank floor
sticky with spirits.

With secrets dark, a woman caresses
her own hand, unknown.
She laughs under
the glare of tawdry teasing.
She looks through the glass
out into the milky shreds of midnight.
A foghorn moans her song,
sung in a swaggering circle
half-lit, guiding her home,
all the way to paradise.

I Am Your Wilderness

You will never tame me, woman.
Wild... WILD... is for the wilderness.
I only visit your beautiful hearth.
You can see my animal eyes over time.
Wild is the visionary bear.
I am stalking the world's dream.
You wait in the certainty called home.
Wild nights of awe and joy call me.
I am the song in your heart, when you awaken alone.

~~~~~~~~~~~~~~~~~~~~~~~~~~~~~~~~~~~~
You... Wild...I... You...Wild... I... You... Wild... I
~~~~~~~~~~~~~~~~~~~~~~~~~~~~~~~~~~~~

Come with me to my sea cliff palaces
draped grand in flags of ferns and mosses.
There's a place for your heart in the wild world too.
Make the crossing and I will come home with you.
But you will never tame me, woman.

Voices

I am their breath
reciting holy names
in the blue sky ink,
through ecstatic strokes.
This desk, this open window,
the cold wind pouring through
my papers, spilling words.
We own nothing in this world.
Tear the pockets off your jacket.
Be possessed by nothing.
Move onto the page
without knowing.
Naked.

The light runs liquid upon this paper.

Listen, let them
in across the page
Alone, within their breath,
for moments.
Let them move
through the house
sweeping away the lint
on the scarred fir
floor, then rising
across the kitchen sink,
then floating out the door.

For moments the voices have
risen. Then they are gone,
just out there, through
the window cold and clear.
Wide open.

We own nothing in this world.
Tear off your pockets and carry
only your breath until
it is time to let that go too.

The Boat
The Lost Poet

Gone now.

Reaching into my heart woods nonetheless.
Between the dew and the fog of a late fall lawn,
between the falling silver sickle and the evening clouds
she sits by me, only a season away.
Writing on the mirrored pond that she loved with her canoe,
at night... only at night...
lit by luminous bodies of birch,
on the far shore.

The body of the earth is
teased by tongues of water,
rolling from the movement of her fragile boat,
sliding into a shadow of stone and secret caves,
moving with her velvet oceans of ink,
on a page of silvered shore.
Water borne.
Water bathed.
Water raised.
Beneath gentle searching fingers.

A night of silence is
flooded in a moon at the edge of vision,
released from time's insistent need for change.
I am bidden by dark eyes,
alive again on this summer night.

She is a season away,
writing from night's muted ink.
She is a rose bowing low
beside a wild mountain lake.
Known in places out of time.
Known by one soul and none.
Known through the gentle ripples.
Rising from her silent craft
in an early autumn twilight.
Moving in signal lines of liquid love.
Rolling upon her lover's luminous skin.
Cool to the touch.
Hungry for eternity.
Waiting for the songs
to fall from her shrouded eyes.
Tracing her memory upon a mirror.

Me, Myself and i

All I really do is talk about myself,
even in the thoughtless purity of moments,
even through the inquiries of how and why,
even with sermons on honoring the earth.
It's all about me,
the proud man
in the cutest broken cottage,
with fourteen dollars left in his wallet.
Me,
railing against the dirt's indifference,
as I crumble away into something more.

Poor Little Mouse

To Her New Boyfriend

I know who you are:
Poor little mouse.
I know what will happen.
Poor little mouse.
I might say I'm happy
for your fate.
But hopes have a habit
of circling back like a hawk.

In a lazy arc, her red tail flaring,
blushing with a lust for blood.
She dives down screaming,
tumbling upon your withered winter field.
Piercing your adoring eyes.
Prey.

It is a dark reunion for you
on a sinking stubbled morning,
when a hungry distance is closed
fast. She is diving into your trembling.
Suddenly she will fall upon you
from heaven.
It will be too late to save
the life you once loved.

Seven Years

For Michael

Seven years ago the Bear
came to me in a huff
of wind falling from her
oaken cave. High up, tumbling
down into the soft red clay
of me. "Come home," she said
in the growling timber-framed sky.
"Come back to your senses," she whispered
from the fluttering heart of a leaf.
"Be still," she cried through
my storm, reckless with winter.

Seven years ago the Bear came.
She licked my face before
she invited me into her den.
She nuzzled my hand with her wet nose
before she rolled into my lap
and tore my guts away.

I see through her eyes now.
Seven years
is just long enough
to be swallowed by the universe.
Seven years,
and I've finally come home,
finally at peace with the tears
that saved me.

Stones

Seven Tons
Building a Stone Wall

The stone people are coming!
We'll be lifting their spirits,
placing their hard
bodies into the soil.
Five hundred hearts of the planet
falling onto the hungry earth,
swallowing them whole,
pulling their songs back
into the darkness where
they were born.

Offering Stone
Given to the Ocean Before a Voyage

I found a stone with a mouth
that told stories of falling into the sun.
The stone had eyes glittering
with a map of the dark earth's riches.
My hand held the stone.
The stone held my soul.
We left all the other maybe lovers behind,
spinning into the wild calm,
sinking, shining and drunk,
down through the dark pearl sea,
into a warm lap, a blanket of stars,
and a thousand songs
waiting to be remembered.

Stuck at Seventeen
Leering in the Mirror

Vile old man
with a cigarette smile and
sour mash sweat.
He sowed your racing heart
with a wandering life, guilty
with his pleasures.
He's the one to
hate, not me.

See the trembling smile.
Taste his words, sour
in your gut, stewed
at seventeen. Lock jawed in
a prison cell of the stars,
an unexplored life,
wandering with unseen feats
of a sad smiling spirit.

You were suckered from security,
shelving surety with pills of happy
smiles pinned beneath the scratching
sweat that sudsy soap could not subdue.
Your sweet seventeen smile
fluttered with the morning tang
of a Marlboro blowing out your brains.

You can't blame
me for the ashen ghosts that swirl
around your sight with the steaming
scent of a singed survivor, gaping
at the sky, strapped to the bars
of a wide open door in the boxcar
hobo home that you won't ever leave.

The Old House Beside the Airbase

Beneath layers of tubes and labels
a 23 year-old boy feels
the shuddering thrill of fire.
He moves above earth and home,
into a freedom we watchers can rarely imagine.
There's a song in the click
of the scuffed red trigger toggle
levitating under his gloved
thumb's quivering.

I feel no power, no transcendence,
just the shudder of my house.

The warrior rises in his jet,
released from his keepers,
released into the morning fog,
searching for targets who have
no names, no faces, no children waiting.
Straight up and hard,
the F-15 flies for only an hour.
In that hour one thumb flick
can ignite a world.

What am I doing at this desk
with sputtering candles? What do I see
through the torn screen filled with spider webs?
I am an old man, earth-bound and aiming
for resurrection. Six a.m., the city stirs slowly in
jet fueled coffee. Every morning I'm here waiting,
watching the young man ascend, raptured
within his titanium god of fire.
I have palsied hands trying to penetrate
the clouds that bind most of us. In an hour,
the smoky boy will fall out of that same ceiling.
I'll still be here. A few pages filled. Maybe
God will speak or maybe the paper
will only be an offering for the fire.

Warriors always fall down
between heaven and asphalt. With me
somewhere in-between the two,
rising with the sun.

Winter, Summer, Inside-Out
The Old Furnace on a Cold Summer Day

The furnace flames sit up with a bolt.
Wham!
The pipes and the old cast iron sides shimmer.
The heat spills out onto the cold floor.
For a month I'd thought summer had come to stay.
I thought the fire was asleep for the season.
Yet today we are jolted awake again by gray winter dreams.
Wham!
The rain isn't done with us yet.

In a week or a month or a decade,
my life will turn inside out.
A fire will rise in a high arc from over the east,
circling the cold hands of fog,
fingering into a mind of hidden coves,
dreaming upon islands at yuletide,
becoming a hearth blazing
in the windows of a humble cabin,
like the eyes of a woman's constancy
holding the warmth for her old familiar,
deep in her pillowed corners of midnight.
Then, on an icy morning like this,
a trembling lover will fling open the window.
Wham!
She'll call back a fire,
cast long ago,
from the wide embracing sky.

Skeleton Keys

The old keys hang on the wall beside the desk
on a summer's cord of jute.
The rust and ring were buried in the basement,
underground for sixty years dark and mute.
Reunited now with a lock painted tight,
for a door shining with twenty layers of blues and green.
For sixty winters, forgotten in the cellar.
Risen to this writing desk where candles shine.
Exploding stars of hearth found flame welcoming them home.
Opening doors once imagined in the cold arms of dirt and root.
Returned in this summer page's spiraled song of inky lute,
buried in a dream until tonight.

The Migration of Desire

Cathexis:
To psychologically incorporate
an object of longing into ourselves.

2005

Returning to School

Her name turns in the twilight.
The fan on the ceiling
weaves her smile,
the shape of her hips,
her arched back in black lace.
I have my reasons
for taking a poetry class
with so many young faces.
Poem is just an exercise to them.

To me, *Poem* is the way she breathes,
the light of her mouth,
the movement of her honest thoughts.
"It's all in the syllabus," she says
at the beginning
of our huddled class.
But it's all right here,
turning in the air
above my bed
soft as clouds and moss,
enfolding this dark cave of blankets.

After class she asks me, "So why are you here?"
"To start at the beginning…again," I say.
She opens the doors to the night,
into the tropical sigh of late summer.
Her hair glides in the Milky Way.
Her smile is the crescent moon.
Her eyes, the Pleiades.
Her arms, branches of swaying magnolia.
Her voice, a night bird calling for home,
fragrant as the trade winds.

Then I breathe her into my night.
Weave her into my dreams.
Turning her over and over into a hope
falling from a lifetime of breaths,
raining through the sieve of stars
in a black lace night.

My poetry lives and breathes in this world!

As she walks into the night
the wind tells the only story
that was ever true and real,
rising with the trembling
moan of the swaying field,
with voices, born again, chanting low:
In the beginning was the Word,
and the Word was with God,
and the Word was God.

A Crush of Ocean over Tea

There was a moment
when your face lit up.
"You're so elfin," you mused,
with smiling eyes, liquid sweet.
Traced on your cheeks
paths of rarely wandered
joy, in an instant
over tea, on a night raining.

Right there,
I wanted to touch
your hand trembling.
I wanted to kiss
the stars in your hair.
I wanted to move you
through the rain-worn window
into the other world
where wandering is art and
swimming sun streams is life.

Will you wander through
the window to the other side
of the rain? Will you
come with me, fairy princess,
angel of the mind, longing
for my earth? Will you
come with me through the sunrise
mirror, caressing a vision
of sky hovering gently
upon my face, adoring you
across the storm-streaked panes of clear
running currents, longing
for the sea, held
in meandering courses
on the journey filled
with dream fish
swimming free.

There's Something in This Pen

There's something in
this pen: a light, the soft
hair of her temple,
streaming lines,
the sky god falling into heaven,
down to earth. There's something
in this pen, new as today is new,
wounded and humming
with a crazed grace, a song
heard on a May morning,
tortured words surrendering
to the light, worshiping,
becoming whole again,
as it was before Eden,
when the sunrise cleansed us,
as her tears flooded
my chest as
the new words of a baby,
not knowing how to ponder,
sensing only the light,
only the breath of her soft
hair singing upon her temple.

The Player

I've been a player,
wandering from hand to hand,
to mouths of soft animal skin,
a player of the harp,
the lute, the slide trombone,
from a band to duo,
playing for dollars
tossed into my guitar case,
walking the streets,
preaching the gospel,
wearing a velvet tie at a wedding,
belting out the top 40 hits,
a player, playing… being played.

It's still morning, just
like it was morning
earlier at 2 a.m.
when I stumbled out
my tangled words
onto her porch
held by vines shivering,
watching Orion
laugh at me
as he fell westward
into the coast range,
his eyes fixed
on the player being played,
like the yawning sun plays
a meadow lark in April,
like the stroke of tides
rising to work the stony shore,
breaking rock into fine pieces.

Who's laughing now, Orion?
Even you hunt in circles,
wanderer of nights.
Who are you
when you finally pierce your quarry,
when you find the sun
rising, your hands

tangled in her autumn hair?
Who's laughing now, Orion?
What music brought you
down to earth
this morning after
a night's ceiling of candlelight stars,
a blue moon and now
the flooding of the sun
through the window,
open again
with a robin's notes falling
upon the pillow, her tongue
warm dew searching
your fields heavy with silence?
Who's laughing now, Orion?
Whose heart is quarry
in the window
hot with stars?
~
I want this:
to know the sun's
tangled flesh rising,
heat of mornings,
ultraviolet sky,
winking breath
sweet with stars
tossed down and dreaming.

I want this:
a band, brassy and jagged,
a harp lowly and sing song,
a tap dance in a brick alley,
a string section dressed in black and white.

I want this:
A duo, birds on the window sill
waiting for the morning,
waiting for the music
they know by heart.

I Want o Die in Your Arms

I want to die
in your arms at the end,
in the beginning of forever. I want
to light our hearth in
our home washed with laughter
and passing tears. I want to marry
the muse inside of you,
face to face, releasing the gods
of the first dawn into your open
doors, lying down beside
you, knowing that
we've had our seasons
sweet and wild.

"Isn't it good!"
we'll say on the last night of summer.

You are God's choice
for me. In the end
when the last poem falls,
I will say it again:
Love is the word between our hands,
the blessing tumbled upon the ground,
shining through the effort of summer,
shed in the patience of fall.
Our love is grace upon the earth.
I rest within you and know myself,
and know something greater than our time
together. Eternity is here!

I want to die in your arms,
every day until the beginning,
every day until we lie down together
forever, born again and again.

Holy Is the Fool
A Man Speaks to the Muse About Their Beloved Woman

I am willing to be a fool for you,
but mostly a fool for us, together.
I will serve the Words, a fool,
his pen deep inside
the world of souls, searching
the tides of the heart.
                    ~
        My beloved's voice is majesty wandering
        out from my holy mistakes, her spirit
        rising with mine, her hand
        touching your face. I will
        be the fool. What else
        is there to be? All the paths
        of figuring and conniving
        led through a chain of broken homes.
        Holy, holy, holy is the fool.
        Holy is the one who stops trying.
        Holy, the one worshipping the Living Word,
        bowed down at Her feet, scrawling
        runes upon the weedy cracks
        of a city street, a fool
        who has lost the sense
        to be afraid, in love,
        witnessing the light soaring
        upon her morning face, happy
        for the first time, happy
        as a fool surrendering
        to waves he cannot outrun.

Details

The morning after she organized a protest march against government policies

I'm not made for politics.
There's a night
in the protest leaving me dark.
What joy is there
shouting and fretting? What joy?
I'm sorry, I'm so selfish at the end
of the world. To be honest
I just want to hole up, dance
with my friends, say the prayers, dream
in the morning, drink my coffee,
and write poem after poem
for desire and island dreams,
for the trees and
for the ocean winds still free to sing.
I want to love you deep and stormy
beneath your eucalyptus tree
that lives five hundred miles north
of its territory, out of place
and season, still thriving and
singing in the city.

I only want to remember your eyes
piercing me. You held my arms
straight out, you hovered above me
as a thunderstorm, full
of lighting and rain, full
of promise and sorrow, full
of destruction and birth, pinning my body,
the shivering flesh rising
even in the fear of the many deaths
my heart has hurtled into. I am
the desert jumbled with steaming
stones and startled trees bent low,
food for the wandering storm.
Your blazing eyes were a mirror
over me. Thunder rolling
across the tired earth, in a room
of the morning's bright shadows. We have no choice
in this sutra of sun and stratus, cumulonimbus,
lightning and arroyos longing for a flood.
Let the rain fall.
Let the cloud hovering, descend.
Let the desert's details lay scattered
throughout this house of open doors.

Heart of the Ocean

I love you
in the deepest
heart of the ocean,
beneath the waves,
beyond the sun, buried
in the crystal embers
of trembling power,
in a bed where dreams are
not just dreams anymore.
I love you
in the dark,
knowing nothing but
the hum of currents,
leaving, arriving, spiraling
in this place beneath
the world with no words or body,
nothing but you, beyond
the storms and sun, floating
above the womb
of the earth, born
moment to moment
by unseen hands and fingers.
I love you
here forever
in the dark
heart of the ocean.

Holy Night

That night, holy
with sage embers glowing
in thirteen rhythms of ghostly
winds within your old house.
O holy night covered in dreamless sleep,
your mouth opening slightly,
the curve of your hips,
your naked arm stretched over my chest,
your soft breath rising in a tangle of feral hair.
That night, awake, caring
more for this remembering than for sleep.
When I'd kiss your eyes,
you'd murmur low,
soft as your skin.
I was happy, one night,
one holy night.

Slot Canyons

On the Eve of Leaving for Santa Fe, New Mexico

She calls in the balm
of early afternoon summer.
"Thanks for being so patient
with me. It's an honor
to go with you on this trip," she says.
Her sweet side is trembling like the clouds
after a downpour. All my pride is washed
into the slot canyon chasm. Forgetting
why I died this morning. Not caring
if I succumb again tonight.
~

Half awake in my dreams at 2 a.m..
Canyons of cans, wet rags,
rusted stoves crowd dark rooms.
I am buried deep. In a panic
I push off the old news-
print. Suffocating me.
"Something's wrong,"
I scream, now sleepless.
Then she reaches under yesterday's news,
kisses me like a flash flood raking the stones.
She stares wide-eyed, the moon
pouring through rain-etched
glass and a torn curtain.

I dream again:
I am a young boy, dancing
his paper kite flying
high in the blue
black face of a storm.

The boy smiles and leaps,
thrilled by the someday promise
behind the smothered sun.
The lightning is making a false day,
 flashing light fleeting as joy
with webbed sheets as powerful as death.
"Go deeper," the ghost wind sings
in the morning shudder. "The waters are rising
in the Sangre de Cristo Mountains."
~
The child dances to the edge
of the stone-faced precipice.
His kite precedes him between worlds,
over the edge of knowing,
in the clean canyon air, hovering
for a moment weightless and free.

Armageddon

We've begun our holy disaster,
falling with the white riders
of God's justice.
Without ever knowing
the garden's delights,
we leapt straight
for the end of the world.
Our bed is a battle field
of blood and seared valleys.
Our letters written as prophecy:
Behold, the end has come.
Prepare ye the way of the Lord.
Laid low by grief,
our bodies are heaped
islands in Megiddo,
old arguments lie rotting,
useless as mangled weapons,
with empty eyes aimed skyward.
Silence now after the war.
Even the crows shun the unholy
wreckage of the unsaid.
Assumed by the Blessed Virgin.
Thrown into Purgatory by Saint Peter.
Avenged by the Archangel Michael.
Pray for salvation
at the end of tears. The bed is torn.
The holy veil in the dark room is smoldering,
ravaged by hopes, unrepentant,
ignoring the ways of nature,
unmoving after three nights in the tomb.

Masonry

Critical words fall
into my lap. I eat
them. I am heavy
with their sand
They are sweet red meat,
souring as they wedge
in my throat, weights
of a hundred bricks
pushing their way
through my pores.
I am a mason
building up another
charming façade, smiling and
swallowing my piece of work whole,
coagulating mortar between blood
ruby desires and the heartbeats
I once named in dreams.

Morning After
5:00 A.M.

Awakening more sober.
The sentimentality is smothered by morning realities.
The rain fell in curtains all night,
the dark dreamless drumming upon my head,
soaking through a halo of memories.

The sun wakens
the eyes of the open window.
Steam is rising from a
silent breath,
silent roof,
silent cup of joe,
silent street littered
with a shattered taillight and a bent stop sign
ruined by a drunken boy who was careening at midnight.

The robin sings again.
The good people turn on their kitchen lights
and wake their soft-throated cars.
The freeway begins to
moan like the breathing sea foam.
The pen scratches the page again.
Rain is falling.

Your Dress

I am mending
your torn dress, which hung
for thirty-three days
over the spine of my bedroom chair.

I am sewing on new pearl bright buttons,
(like your eyes)
restretching the web of lace
that once framed the arch of your back,
ironing the collar that held the wild sunset
swirling in your hair.

I am hanging up
your dress, clean as our one
spring entwined.
Your dress, the color of fallen leaves
(like your eyes)
of an All Hallows Eve sky hanging low.

I have closed
the closet door that holds
your dress. Your pleats,
now in the arms
of my plaid farmer's shirt
stained with mud,
in the dark place
behind the sliding trick mirror,
a dusty museum.

I will open your memory
every quiet morning
when I begin my day.
Then I will close
(like your eyes)
the door at night,
to dream of our fall and
the spring that will never come again.

A Whole Life

Did we live a whole life
together in spring?
Is ours a love sustaining
me for the lifetime without you?

Is it possible to marry,
raise three children,
grow small and gray and
die in a bed shared for only one season?

Truths are alive in their time.
Our May has been thrown into July.
Will we remember our rising suns
and forget the rains of June?

Wait on the other side.
Time is our circle.
It will not be long.
Wait for another
life to flood our bodies.

Time is the river closing
our eyes with sleep and dreams.

Washing the Dishes

When does it ever end?
Washing the dishes,
head down, hands warm and scrubbing,
crying for you, sweet baby,
washed up, spiraling down the drain.
Cold blood rinsed clean away.
Crying for you, sweet baby.
Your face in the milk,
mocking me in the steel curves,
the fickle flickering splashes
of your eyes,
down deep,
the plates,
the drain.
Your words
are whispers wiped away.
Spinning the brush in circles.
Your hair,
the soap,
the bowls clanking,
a drowning bell clanging,
going through the motions,
breathing in circles.
Cleaning up and going through it,
around and around again.

She Writes of a Man Far out at Sea

She is writing a book
of secrets, stones, and storms.
He lives inside her
black-bound soul,
tracing her words on the face of the water,
listening for her voice
in the lines,
in the wind rising,
in a head full
of the ocean's deep nights
far out at sea.

She is a watchman of memory,
wandering in the black village vaulted
overhead, the mast singing
with the spray, salted and
cold, beckoning him into the tides
deep into himself, into a room rocking,
where he no longer cares
for his idle thoughts in shallow gulfs.
He is the rain, whipped
with the primal remnants
of an old cyclone that once raged
on a long-ago coast.

He is bound
for the open sea.
His soul is soaring
above the village of silent watchers,
the slow fire of the current burning,
in a storm. Far out at sea,
between the ghost fish swimming and
the moon's eye gazing,
knowing not his own name,
sensing the ways secreted alight
in the spray and star-strung foam.
He is the green shimmering within
her pages of distant feral winds,
where dreams waken from days
slipping into night's liquid arms.

She Writes...

He is flying
on the open sea
beneath the wind's rushing hands,
delirious with death's drowning promise,
resurrected in the deep vaults, secreted
away in her pages of white foam rising
in blues and pearls.

He is falling
into the ocean, overflowing
with hidden travelers.
He stands watch with them,
memorizing their songs for tomorrow
on the other shore,
behind the ink moon horizon,
in a flood tide of recollection
of the waters alive,
ebbing with a forgetting sigh.
The winds rain in a circle
strung between the stars and the heart
of the earth far below,
beyond the voices of the gale.

~

She is alone with the man at sea,
open as the wave mouth
crying out into a fist of clouds:
"Fill me; I am thirsty!
Wash me; I am dark as the night."

She is writing her book
filled with the waters
of heaven's night, forgetting,
cleansed with the spray
upon his sails
taught by the cold night voices
of the searing wind.

A Thief Bringing Gifts in the Night

She creeps
into my chest, hidden.
When I am unaware,
she rummages
through old movie
reels and leaves them playing
on my projector in a dark
room where the curtains are
dusty and drawn.

Sometimes I walk
into that room
longing for a familiar quiet stillness,
to rest in my overstuffed chair.
When I lie down, I am struck
to see our life playing
upon the blank wide wall.

"Could have been," I say
as I stand and stumble back
toward the door,
its heckling hinges laughing.
I turn to look one
more time before
the latch clicks.

I lean into the wooden body,
a closed door
between us, still listening
to her voice in the make-believe
of a sad-sacked cinema,
filled with a soundtrack of murmuring laughter,
wafting with the smell of day-old popcorn and
the shadows of acned kids making out
in the back row corners.
Ghosts play upon the screen
beneath a false summer sun
in a dancer's hair.

There is a moaning winter wind
stumbling through the hallway now
in our fallen cottage of whitewashed honeymoons.
It's just make-believe on the other side
of the hard swung door.
It's only my life waiting
on the other side
in the flickering night.

Detour on the Road to Abiqui, New Mexico

We never made it
to Abiqui. Our trail
of tears ended in Gallop.
O'Keefe's rosy succulence must wait.
Our destination is resigned to a folded map.
For the two of us, only the dust
of Laguna's nuclear wheeze.
For us, the Sky City is impenetrable.
For us, reservations
for a honeymoon casita bypassed,
a sunrise in a hand-hewn room
we'll never see.

We're flying home early,
a love aborted in early summer,
when the heat lies
low in the mesquite
and the river runs
dry before it can tumble
into the stony heart
of Abiqui.

The Fallen

2006

Rain is falling from my pen.
I am a bright sky
full of clouds.

Whispering Through the Door

Consider our home:
The spider on her web,
hoping for entanglements
in the clear clean air,
the tufted nest
of the stallion sparrow
singing to a deaf sun,
the old woman next door
rising with the cracking shock
of every car door slamming,
the family of four on the corner,
each in their own room
watching their own shows,
the dapper gray man working
at night in the neighborhood
he's known since birth,
the boy sleeping in late, rising
every morning to a quiet breakfast.
Our world is built
upon an altar of solitude,
each being in our own thoughts,
weaving in the air
a shivery web to catch the wind.

If you knew God was at the door,
the light beating in His chest,
if you heard Him whispering your name,
His lips pressed into the door frame,
if you awakened to the squeaking rock
of the swing on your front porch,
would you change?
Would you peer through
the faded curtain and smile?
Would you whisper back
the words you caught in your web?
Would you open the door?
Would you discover the truth
about our lives together?

Lavender Oil

I am the scented oil
poured into your open hands.
I move through your quivering
fingers and am wiped away,
leaving just enough
of me to adorn
your body
with a whisper of pleasure.
Then I am gone, sunk
into the floor, seeping
into the deep wells
of your skin.

Planetary Bodies

I orbit you.
I am your moon
gazing upon your brilliant continents,
never touching,
falling around
instead of falling into
you.

Our gravity is building,
bringing the collision
that will obliterate our worlds,
scattering us to the ethers.

Inseparable.
Diffuse.
Travelers.
Together.

Becoming a billion stars,
newborn and primal.
Flying from the catastrophe
that longing could not refuse.
Crossing the border
into a universe larger than hope.
Moving in the arc of a spiral,
closer and closer
to the center of everything,
closer and closer
to the light that is our home.

Addiction to Heaven

I needed
the grand staircase
to paradise,
the dramas of ecstasy,
the denial and oblivion,
the drug of someday.
God's cells wept
within my body.
I needed the fix
of somewhere better
until I came to you, my wife
with dirt under your fingernails
hair strewn gray as
the winter shock of morning.
Your eyes watching
a fool who was
dismissing this world, a man
who tried to climb into heaven
when it had fallen into heaps
all around him.

What You Do

That's just what you do.
You're beside her when she's sick at 1 a.m.
You're driving her home from the surgeon's office.
You're listening as she recites the reasons she cannot love you.
You love her anyway.
That's just what you do.

3:10 A.M.

I woke myself up, moaning
in the place between
dreams and sunrise.
I could not move.
Paralyzed when I heard
a voice of the dead:
Darling, are you there?
Hello, are you awake?
I could not tell.
I could not speak.
I could only moan in reply.

Tooth Fairy

It is the time after.
The moon has fallen.
The sun dreams of rising.
~

The man is awake,
with shallow breaths,
alert in another world,
hearing the footsteps
in the hallway,
the teasing groan of the door
coming unhinged,
as the pink light of the passage
oozes inward.
A shadow marks him,
with that hand reaching out
tentative and trembling.

"You're so handsome."
the voice says,
in another night,
before morning
mounted the verdant earth.

He makes himself into
a black broken root.
He becomes
an invisible shade
curled beneath the pillow.
He is the tooth pulled,
waiting for the fairy's hand
to snatch him away,
exchanging him for a pocketful
of well-rubbed quarters,
each with a stone-faced man
and eagles wings splayed
wide open and flightless,
shining beyond the musky shadow
floating above him.

To My Wife

I'd use it all up
to be a pauper,
to revel
in the gift of hunger,
to awaken
in your hand
time and time again.

I'd sell everything but my soul,
and that I would place upon your lips,
a trembling gift,
the breath of a poem
that lives forever
in a moment.

Love Has a Body

Love has a body all its own.
The spirit may fly.
The mind will fade.
But the body hangs on
years since the first
signs of illness arose.
The body fights to survive,
thirsts for its one and only life,
struggles for the right to breathe
one more breath.

Autumn

Summer sun
splashed upon
melting forests.

In This Season...Terrible Beauty

Watching Orion rising at 2 a.m.
O, what terrible beauty...
the consolation
of being awake.

Grass in the Wind

"Behold, I am the wind!"
she chanted with a flourish,
hands raised in praise,
back arched like a siren
culling the clouds.
Now she truly is the wind,
weaving through my fingers
as I lay back to back
with the earth. I smile
in the green dew light singing:
"Behold, I am the grasses swaying."
And soon enough I will be
        dancing with the wind.

Hospice

You lay on your side.
Fetal.
Hair in pink ribbons.
Eyes fixed.
A haze, smoking in the cave of your heart...
the shelter I'd stumbled into a thousand times.
You were mute.
Remember our songs?
Your skin was paste slipping from beneath
a mountain of blankets.
The window was cracked an inch,
with the winter breathing in and out.
You flew about the room.
No one else noticed how your spirit rose
into the spheres, circling a bright singing tree.

Ah, love, how can life be so cruel and death so vain?
Who are you now?
A dozen photographs...
a sweet face crying on the water's edge,
earth's brown eyes watching from the fire lookout,
a laughing woman in circle we called family?
Who can know my grief,
now that you are dancing around the great tree?

The Neighbor

Something sad has happened
in the house across the street.
A single light was on when I arrived
home an hour before sunrise. A figure,
dark as death with her scythe,
sat in the stiff shadows, erect,
except for her face bent and frozen.

We watch the same
dawn's light and ice rising.
The morning melts the rime
in the bird bath. The rose buds dream.
The street sparkles like the Salish Sea.
Across the street her lace curtain
shudders from some internal storm.
I can feel the squall, like I can feel the groaning
of our world's ice beneath my shoes.
Her husband's car has been absent
for a week. Her silence is
brooding with pagan keens,
her hands clasping her face,
her eyes wide as the clouds
watching me
watching her,
sharing the camaraderie
of tears unshed.
Both of us frozen inside.
Both of us considering vows
that must be broken, waiting
for new life wrapped within
sheaths once green.

Clever Poets

This is all very clever stuff,
words wedged in just right,
illuminating some thought-filled
story. O clever poets,
don't you understand? This
breath is the poem!
The story moves in your veins.
Be nothing more
than alive. Be still.
You are nothing
more or less than the song
you try to weave into patterns.
There's sense in it all,
when you feel the Word
wrapped around you as a blanket.
O poets, be still.

We walk
into the fire.
We live
in the burning.
We fly
within the smoke.

The Working of the Winds

2007 – 2008

Old Apple Tree

Two ravens call to me
and circle the sun.
I rise through
shimmering limbs.
No thoughts.
No reasons.
The dancing of the branches,
the swaying of the fruit,
the working of the winds...
these are real.

Dreamer, the Winged Have No Hands

Would you exchange
your hands
for wings?
What loss comes
with flight?
What joy
with soaring?
Why do angels
have both
fingers and feathers?
And why must we
of the earth
choose between
the two?

Empty Nest

He's the bachelor sparrow swaying
in the tufts of a fine round nest.
Hoarse, dream bound from singing.
But it's Autumn and no gray dame has come.
The time for singing has passed.
His flock wheels toward the sun of Mexico.
It's too late for warmth.
This soft home mocks him,
with an empty mouth open and begging,
the sky cold and chaotic.
His dying tree is succumbing to a million falling stars.

My cottage is bright with mums and
geraniums that cling to summer
with their reds and whites.
Fine Berber carpet is freshly laid. Burgundy
swags sway in the sunny windows. Gentle
tunes spiral within the breeze. A linen lace
table welcomes two chairs and candles bright.
Only one chair is pulled back.

Forest Fire
The Castle Rock Complex in Central Idaho
August 2007

Something has been released.
Something has been taken.
Something has been offered.
A part of the body cries. A wisp
of hope hovers in mid-air, gasping
for earth. An old wooden
span has snapped.
The house, once shiny,
moans on her foundations.
Do you feel the pressure plummet?
An opening for the storm drops in
from the desert through the charred flanks
of once glacial rivulets.
The house knows her fate from the creaking
of the ceiling and the shuddering
of panes and jams.
Prepare ye the way for Holy Karma,
Destroyer, Creator
of changing winds,
lover of smoky offerings.

Christmas Shopping

I went Christmas shopping
on the night she died.
Later,
I threw all of her gifts
away,
mistaking them
for trash.

The Publisher's Festive Party

It wasn't the pretentious pompous pretenders
that brought me low at the party.
It was me, thinking it is a sin
to be afraid of superficial jingoisms,
to live in between the starry sky burned by the sun's joy and
the muddy pile of my own archeological despair.
I just listened to the chat and chit.
When a clever eye caught mine, I'd laugh,
clutching my fine wine,
eventually happy with the person I am,
cradling the spirit I cannot contain.

The Soft Parts

I was
neither male
nor female.
Not boy.
Not girl.
Not gay.
Not straight.

I was a machine
for your service,
for your pleasure,
at your bidding.
I was androgynous,
circuits and gears
and soft parts…
always the soft parts
betraying your steely
hands.

I was your mechan-ism,
I-robot,
an alien,
glazing over
to a touch,
no deeper than
your wanting.

I never felt
my animal body.
I was only springs
and pulleys.

Finally the soft parts
gave up on your
power over me.
The soft parts
brought me home,
as a real human being,
alive for the first time.

Morning Coffee

"Sugar or milk with your coffee?" I ask.
You shine to me your deep mocha worlds.
Your eyes are my singing stars.
You answer with your mouth close to mine.
"You know, only crème."
So I pour out my dreams:
the fine white fire of your skin
as you sleep, the flooding
oceans when we fall into each other,
the way of silence when another day is
borne from the hole in my heart.

The Tryst

"This is going to be very interesting." she said as she laid her
blouse neatly on the chair's hard haughty back. She looked out
the bedroom window. The sun was rising to the hum of the
freeway. He watched her from the safety of blankets and pillows.
Covered. She shivered when she released the clasp hidden behind
the flower on her bra. She sent her socks flying with the flick of
her feet, one chasing the other to the floor. One by one she shed
the numbers of her perfect equation.

She looked out the window again, remembering the bells on
Sunday morning and the fog of rocky shore line. She knew what
life had in store for her way back when. She knew.

Her hands hesitated as if to give the rest of her body the chance to
reconsider. Then she laced her fingers through the noose of her
belt. Everything she knew, the fabric of common sense, all the
bright colored dreams, warm and supple, fell into a heap. She
turned her head, her gaze pulled into his eyes, enticing her
downward.

Creation Myth

You made a story out of me
with those figures you conjured
out of the muddy field,
breathing the past into the ooze.
You gave them a life of their own.
You are the goddess
who shapes reality
from clumps of clay
made in your own image.
How can a mere mortal
argue with your truth?

We Walk on Graves

Everyday, Everywhere, Everyone

Remember this.
We walk
upon the graves
of our ancestors,
and the creatures now shy
of sun and sound.
Everywhere we tread
a life has been borne.
All of the sleepers
once like us.

I wonder if they feel
me walking above
their stony beds?
I wonder if I will
make my descent
into the grass with ease?
Will it be lonely,
the time after today,
when I hear the footsteps
above my empty chest?
Who remains?
Who waits for me
in the secret world?

Wearing His Heart on His Sleeve

Razors and needles,
an open vein cut
to the quick,
a tough spirit
softened in the hidden
places.

There's a reason
he wears hot shirts,
long, and gripping
his wrists, hiding
blood.

After the screaming,
he wraps up in
sticky
white
tape to hold himself
together.

There's a sleeve of skin
where his heart wells up
in sacred pools,
a carnation sacrifice
drying up, nailed
to the dark face
curdling in his cold
bedroom.

His body is a spongy plank
that barely holds the weight
of his boiling
brain.

The feather of a blade bends
into the milky sweet soil of sinew,
bringing down the mind,
spinning in circles.
Finally he feels real pain.
He is no longer
just a spirit hovering
in the night.

Devastate Me

Devastate me with
the light of your eyes.
Destroy me with
the touch of your hand.
Steel me with
the rising of your body.

I am the whole
universe now,
beloved awakening
my blood.

I am the waves
upon the stormy sky.
I am the bending
low of cedar.
I am the white flame
hidden between the mountains.

Devastate me with
your adoration.

My arms,
are wide with wind and starlight.
My heart,
is the flood of summer rain.
My hand,
is melting in your hand.

Sometimes a Ghost

I suspect I am a ghost.
Suspicious of all that is supposed to be real.
Still longing to be a part of it all.

Nights I awaken and feel a woman's heart beating.
Though I left consciousness in the twilight alone,
she is now sleeping beside me.
I came back through her darkness. Perhaps
she is the one living in flesh and time, and
I am her apparition. Perhaps
this house belongs to a new owner. Perhaps
all that I consider solid is a dream
from the other world. Perhaps
I may really be dead,
doing my chores,
riding my motorcycle too fast,
drinking in the smoke with other ghosts,
haunting the world of humanity,
barely felt as a cold shiver
to the woman climbing into her winter bed.

I wonder about ghosts
and all the other shades
in this world.
Do you hear their whispering?
Do they also begin their day,
frying eggs in bacon fat and floating
in the steam of fresh coffee? Perhaps
they see a flicker at the edge of their table,
not knowing it is me:
the one thinking
I'm also real in the world.

Mountain, River Bed

~~

~~~~

You've carved
a well-worn river
bed into my arm.
In this dry season
the channel is deep and ragged,
full of thoughts and memory.
When the rain falls
on your distant mountains,
I am full of your eyes
shining my love.
Flood me,
my dark
mountain fairy,
beloved.
Flood me
again and
again.

~~~

~~

~

From your lodge
on the dark mountain,
where I cannot go,
speak to me softly.
Let the cloud's night fall
from your mouth.
Shatter the sky
with my name.
Cry above this world,
down canyons
of carved skin.
In this desert place
send one word,
my name,
the rain
quenching the thirst
of this bright
dry season.

No One in the House But You

Don't assume you know how she feels.
She may even be courting another lover.
Who knows?
Do you base truth on a full hug of phone calls?
Assuming is entertaining.

What is real?
What is true?

You are in a play put on stage between your ears (and other parts).
The actor is an empty heart behind the orchestra pit.
You are the observer with your memories in the bone auditorium.
There's no one else in the house but you.

The Comforter

I am your favorite old jacket,
the one with the pills of wool,
a splash of yesterday's wine,
elastic stretched into strings.
I am the comforter, the holy spirit
hovering over you in the morning,
the garment you reach for
before your coffee or curtains.
I am surrounding you when your schemes
wander into the daily chores
you consider to be so important.
Some things become known and
loved even if they're seldom really seen.

Defeat
Ode to Rilke

The defeat by greater beings makes us real.
It's not the victories that make one into a man or a woman.
It is the pummeling by the angels who deem us worthy.
Wrestling in the sweaty dust, often in public.
There is no shame in being without titles.
That is the reality of all things in the end.
Challenge what you cannot possibly defeat.
Turn from your childhood mirrors and
face the cold laugh of starlight.
Pray for sunrise and kneel.

You are alive.
You are not the name you've made.
You are the sparkling dust
of midnight molded by the gods' hands.
Surrender to that making, the dirty work
of mistakes and hidden inspiration.
Lose the shape that is already melting in the morning dew.

Sleeping and Waking

We slept completely
tangled together,
skin to mouth,
arm draped
across my chest,
hair wild
upon my shoulder.

We slept
in the crumpled heat
with the fan tracing
lazy circles on the ceiling.

Pillows and fingers,
breath and the moon,
rising at dawn,
then silence
deep in the folds
of your inner landscape,
leaping and dancing
in the dream of the spirits.

Waking
your eyes.
Waking
your pulse.
Waking
your hand
soft and slow.

So, let the sun come.
Let the day begin.
Let the curtains open.
Let the door close behind us.
You, to your work.
Me, to my words.

Let it come.
Let it rise.
Let it be.

Was there life
before you?
Was there ever
a morning
like our sunrise?

Imagine a Life

There you were
walking through the front door.
Standing in line for your latte.
I watched you from the back
rumble of our coffee shop.
You didn't see me.
You were just here
for your fix of mortality,
forgetting how you shouldn't
be in this world,
forgetting how I still imagine a life, now
buried in the grounds beneath the grass
steaming in the sunrise.

Full of the Islands

I'm full of the islands and ocean today.
A whisper of longing rises, pungent
on the sea wrack and mists singing.
I am the ocean today,
her mountains breaking through the waves,
feeding the sky, her womb
deep and mysterious. I am the Raven
wind dancer, courting the beloved
who waits between the edges of the tide line.
I am the love of the gods, their gazes
so full of joy that the waters rise up
to meet them.

There is *my* space, *your* space and *our* space.
And there are praises for the world, filling
everything within and without. Perhaps
you have been touched by the ocean.
You may have even seen the cabin, shining
with firelight, on the dark island. Secretly
you have hovered with me
in the place that is no place at all.
It's a mystery.

It's Not
The Affair and Your Death

It's not the guilt of betraying my family or yours.
It's not the shame of having broken all the nice guy rules.
It's not even the inner-directed anger about how I left you.
It's the loss of knowing what we might have become.
It's the empty filling of days between
what we forgot and what we attempted.

It's not so much the loss in the past.
It's the future of missing you.

It's knowing that you left in late Autumn
after a Summer of me finding myself.
It's living incomplete
without knowing you here.
It's filling my hands with pleasure
and not raising the sparkling liquid to my lips.
It's how my longing leaked away
between my fingers like tidal sand.

I regret that I never saw it through.
I regret that I was not reckless enough.

Anyway, you're gone and I'm here.
What I know of us now has no right
to be in this world.

Robert's Legacy

I walk straight up
in the rain. No longer
rushing or crouching
in the deluge
like a frightened animal.
You've seen them.
It's instinct.
The wet cool sky falling makes
even the brave shrivel and shirk,
head pulled in like a turtle's humped shell.
The heavy shawl of heaven shrinking the body.

What good is the effort
of resisting the rain?
The icy fingers find their way
through the seams and the collar
no matter the stance.
Now I stand taller
in the deluge. My face
wet and cold,
open as the wind,
letting it fall,
letting it be
what it is.

Buying the Farm
A Summer of Poems

2009

Elysium Fields

This open window facing
south. My spirit
hovering in the rain-light.
Outside, the remnant
field of a once forgotten farm.

An angel took me
to heaven in the dark
season of my boyhood,
then brought me back
to earth
as a man
on this farm,
facing this meadow.

See the rows
of apple and plum.
Smell the heady grasses bent
along the fence line
with rain.
Hear the metal gate
swinging its rusty sing song.

For unnumbered years
only ghosts walked through that gate.

Fingernails of rain
are tapping
on the window.
Yesterday's dreams are breathing
in the yawning grass. The robin is
listening for a morsel
squirming just beneath
the earth's surface.

Elysium is there,
somewhere just outside.
My boyhood sleeps
hidden beneath
the curiosity of the robin.

Let the old longing
fall with the rain,
greening the empty pasture,
feeding the wrinkled cottonwood.
Let the storm
rise from the ocean faraway,
falling now on holy ground.

Ten Billion Years

Ten billion years before
I touched you
we were particles
from seven blazing suns
now dark. Our puzzle pieces
once hidden in the planets
were hung on sound
strings, exploded.

Brought here now,
you and me entering
the enveloping
midnight of one body,
flying in the star shine
of God's eyes.

So many eras.
So many rebirths
for this moment,
fitting together,
proton and electron,
nova and satellite,
infinite pieces shifted
from primal energy.

Let us be
one more exploding sun,
one more burning nebula.
Let us explore the secret
universe, once more
to be a twin star.

Juniper, Grass, and Salt

There is the tang
of juniper and the perfume
of prairie grasses. There is
the sea. And there is me,
here without you.

There is a channel you must
cross to be with me.

I came to your desert island.
You must come soon to my farm,
before the tides go against us,
before I turn
my face from the winds,
before the ocean
of green earth
moans our names
in a lovely story
of unrequited longing.

Holy Things

Holy things show
themselves through surprise:

Like the island rising
over the shoulder of the road
when I was lost

Your glowing
face at the airport
curb

This white farmhouse
I'd passed by
for years

A poem tipping over
the edge of dawn, before
the newspaper hit the driveway

The perfume of the river
as we flew our open
windows across the bridge

Sunlight splashing
as crystal upon
our breakfast table

A covey of quail
in the quivering
snowberry bush

The foghorn
I heard two hundred
miles from the sea

The home I dreamed
of moments before
I woke in your arms.

Through the Heat

It's a day steeped in flames
where the rusty dog no longer barks,
where the tap tap tap of the sprinkler
offers its reward in a song from childhood.
It's the hot of shuttered houses,
the hot of bright clothes bleached
pale and limp on the clothesline.
The burning eye of smoke from the dying forest
adds a paralyzing drug to the dream of the afternoon.
The boiling moon rises in ripples unquenched.
Deer panting in faint breaths are
moving down the canyons in search of the withering pond.

Draped beside the apple tree,
my lover observes a cooler country
on the other side
of the sun. She gazes up
through the branches heavy with fruit.
Her hand anchored to the back of my neck,
sweat conducting lightning between our skin.
The smoke rises as she conjures up the moon,
her burning fingers trembling in my hair.

Smoke

The dearly departed
ghosts of a California
forest float in our sky.
The houses and dreams
of ten million creatures
hang in my nostrils.

Blood orange winds,
a sky root of the Great
Mother Tree withers.

Between the lovers and
users of earth
are the animals and plants.

Here we are
in the middle
with them.

Pray to God
for courage. Pray
to his wife,
the Earth, for mercy.

Renovation

The gray man makes music
with a ratchet, spanner, and wire stripper,
searching with his flashlight
for leaks, cracks, and petulant valves.

The old poet pays
off his longing while fixing
the limping sigh of the furnace fan.
He sweats out his joy in deep
ditches, diagnosing a rotten water main.
His inspiration lingers upon a dusty farm
dog next door, barking thorough
the inky forest.
His reward is an achy
sleep and the dream driven
by making life
better for everyone else.

What is downtrodden is not
ruined forever.

The poems will come
again, some day. Yet
today his ocean song
is the whoosh of the dishwasher, and
the rattle of the ancient
tractor in the field
as he cuts spring's green
growth down to size.

Our First Night in the Old Home

For Pearl

We slept in the pile of the living
room. The farm house, a silent cave.
The coyotes howling outside.
The breath of the early morning dew.

And a visitor:
An old woman stood above us,
and watched us awaken.
She was gray as winter,
long hair, nightgown, sleepy-eyed,
shocked to see us here.
She held her palsied hand to her lips.
Her eyes both surprised and accepting.
"Oh my. I must be dead," she whispered.
Then she faded into the night.

Yes, my dear, you are dead.
I sit by your prized window
watching your silver barn turn
to rust in the June sunrise.
The descendents of your robins
still hunt with the quizzical cock
of their heads. Your peonies
unfold and shimmer like your eyes
when you were young and in love.
Your field still rolls
in green waves with the wind.
And your chipped sink still draws
out visions with the splash and
clank of dishes.

I'm guessing you noticed the wall
I tore out between
your kitchen and the rest
of your house. Your kitchen was
so much like a cage.
Now it's splayed wide open.
Now the wind frolics,
above the wild dog's song.
Children run through
your house laughing.

You, wrinkled matriarch,
are free to go. Thank you.
Fly through the openings
we have made.
The moon is waxing.
Go to the light tearing
apart the darkness.

We'll trim your roses,
scythe your field. Soon
enough we will follow you
into the singing field.

Revisiting the Grave

Your stone grove
is a cold song
of forest shadows.
No heat there.
No heart.
Only the forever
of changing tides
clinging to the skirts
of your island.

How far I've come
from our sea.

Tell me,
even in whispers:
How can my life be
a **Yes!** today?

How do I breathe in
the blazing world
before the cool clay of earth
is my home too?
How do I sing
the secrets
of the ocean
in a dry and rocky land?

Summer Solstice

We made the farm our home,
this week, on the peak of light.
The power of the full
moon blazing white shadows,
sun burning through
our window without curtains.
The couch is our only bed,
where her sleeping breath sings
to the turning folds of my dreams.

At dawn
we awaken.
I am a tidal wave, inundating
her heart with thoughts
and schemes, fierce
with intentions
to make this place
safe with the green
smiles of the field,
dreaming of the future
forest we will plant.

If paradise were
this close,
if love grew
without guile,
then heaven would be
our earth.

Between the shock of barking dogs
and the pull of crying children
are moments of forever.
In the morning field,
the raven's song ruffles
softly upon the young
rabbit's ears. The Sun lounges
upon His zenith throne.
The storming clouds are asleep
upon the sea. Our family is
at rest, miles away from
the rushing waves.

Promise of Rain

Lighting the Old Stove

Reborn,
the old wood stove
hisses and moans.
Years of neglect rise
pungent off the ceramic
skin. Through the coal
stained looking glass,
a yellow flame beats again
as a drum, a drum
a drum a drum a drum a drum
in the center of my chest.

It's mid-morning.
The rain is falling at last.
The islands floated away in my last night of sleep.
My love wanders to work in her silences.
I am here now,
light burning.

The blue veins of
smoke rise from the chimney, then
change their path to hover
among the grasses.

This simple flame is sufficient
for a prayer. This cracked window
is enough for a vision. Outside,
the heavy fields are
wet with promise.

All Night the Storm

All night the storm,
the gods orgasmic
in the mists. Sheets
of lightning, crumpled
clothes of trees thrown
about carelessly. The body
of the river glistening
sweat in the pounding.
Tears falling in
torrents in the end.

The air is pungent with power.
I lie in the dark flashing with thoughts
in ever-tightening circles.

My world of dreams is becoming concrete
while the outside world is being crushed
into ice shards, then melting
into a slurry of oozing clay.

The sacred Earth is knocking
on my back door, talking through the keyhole saying:
"Soon enough the storm will set you free."

Thunder swirling around
this tired old cabin reaches into me.
It's an art to create
a pummeled order from the elements,
just as the thunder is winnowing its way
through me now.

How many dark souls wrote of the wide and wild sky of storms
from one small room?

How many dreamers had the gift to remake that same small space
into a whole world?

Twilight on the Mountain Road

Bright eye moon, veiled in
the spinning wool of clouds.
Vapors hissing and burning
at sunset. Rain drops,
heavy with yesterday's trade winds,
falling upon our windshield.

We sat in the car,
shedding the snake skin
of our mountain road.
Sky flinging her scarlet
hair. Her whispering tunes
dancing in the winds.
Her rising breath weaving
through the shaking trees.

We took photo after photo
through the side window, trying
to collect the light and rain.
Then the scrutiny of the lens was put
away. We held hands.
We held our breaths. We lifted
right out of the gaping windows.

Our lives as we knew them
were over. The fortress
of clouds was falling all around us.
The ramparts melting.
Our home revealed
through the silence
beyond walls.

Perhaps this is too holy
to explain here.

There are moments
when heaven becomes earth,
when lovers become
sun-spun vapors of twilight.
Spirits.
Not quite separate anymore.
Quiet.
The horizon alive with
ruby flames shimmering
through the waves
of ridge stone and mountain fir.

Baby Bird

Darling, you kiss
my zip-locked lips
with an open
wanting mouth.

Baby bird,
I am tired,
with no more
to give.

Our nest is piled
with family resentments,
heaped everywhere with
gaping boxes full
of broken utensils and
unread cookbooks.

What kind of hunger have I taken
on, little bird? Our home
is a cage for the free.
I just want to fly through
the plate glass window.
So what if it breaks
the boundary with clarity,
shattering the panels sandwiched
with dead air.

At the Dance in the City Without You

The dancing was a writhing sweat,
with women watching and searching.
One looked like you,
though younger.
Her desert eyes were
deep and lonely when
meeting my oceanic glances.

I turned away from her,
remembering that you're home
with the children while I danced
free, a man all in black
pretending to be
of the city,
while the country claims me
now with coveralls and sawdust,
sickles in alfalfa,
roosters at dawn, and
a tattered cat scratching
at the barn door.

The city eyes now
turn north, drinking in starry nights
as we sip beer on the back porch.

You and I are
the dancers in the dark mantle
that hovers above our orchard,
we the committed,
we the field
and the freeway home.

Summer Is Waning

Summer is waning.
And you come back
like you left… an Autumn surprise.
I was dreaming you back from
the dead. There you were,
sitting in the alcove
of my cabin, darling woman.
Gone now for five years.
My childhood friend,
you've returned from your island ground.
We talked about what our life
would be like, now
that you were alive again.

You and me and my family,
living
all together.
Strange comfort, even to my new lover,
now that you breathe again,
smiling in the coffee breeze sun,
gleaming in the hand prints
smudged on the cabin window.
Why do you haunt us?
Please stay.

My beloved flits about
in the house across the field,
happy, a stranger
in this world. She has
her sister back home,
her shadow, her doppelganger.
Now we're all together.

My soul has come home.

Two Minds

I want to be the poem
Raven sings as He twirls me in his talons.
I want to be the drunken darkness
winging my way through the thighs
of fir trees and the pebbled streambed.

I want to float in the Raven's eyes,
pushing through to the other side
of the woodland, exploding
into a brand new horizon
full of tawny golden light
dancing on waves of ocean grasses.

But this is an imperfect morning.
This lawn is a battlefield of the moles.
The black dog is barking at gathering clouds.
The alder tree is broken and leaning over the fence line.
The leaking roof is sending its finger of stain onto fresh paint.
The floor is tilting on the broken foundation.

I write in the dust on my desk,
drinking yesterday's coffee and dirty cream,
with an idea of a working wage floating in the mug.
There are dog-eared books splayed on the crumpled bed.
Up from the dangling stereo speaker scratches out a song:
"Returning, returning to the land of your soul..."

Here my soul stands, planted.
Here I write for the dark spirits and the bright.
Here I am for the love of gods and mangled earth.
Here I am listening to the truck rattling down the highway,
watching the cottontails grazing on well tended lettuce,
Raven wheeling sky bound,
cat drowsy on the back stoop.
Here is the sun lighting up the crack
in the ancient window.

The field is still
except for a single blade of grass,
its seed head bent heavy and low,
swaying rhythmic and slow.

What If

What if you really believed
the universe is here to support you,
and even to be enhanced by you?
What if there was a middle way
between the trinkets of consumption and
the sacrifice of selflessness?

Everyone's needs could be met.

What if you were so humble in spirit
that you woke up to inherit the world?
What if you trusted your heart,
opened your mind
and released the heavy load?
What if you wrote a prayer
with your life,
held the hand of the Earth's gift to you,
lived prosperously,
gave generously,
breathed deeply,
slept quietly,
created richly?

Look, the sky is blazing blue
between the clouds and the geese arcing high.
The sun and rain are dancing together.
The corn is swelling sweet with honey.
The cat is asleep at your feet.
All is as it should be.
We've come this far.
Now step through the clouds.

There's a choice to be followed.
It's one way or another.
One is on your knees bent
on shards of stone.
The other is on your knees bent
in the field swaying with song.

Soak in the blue flame of sky.
Fall into the deep green.
Be rewarded in the letting go.
There are only moments
before we leave this palace
of breath and wonder.

The sun is gold in the corn.
Last night's rain is glistening
like a million stars.

About the Author

Rick lives beside a verdant field and forest with his family in Southwest Washington State. He tends a humble sustainable farm that serves local farmer's markets and neighbors. He is an artisan, providing workshops on drum making and contemplative writing practices. He is also an ordained minister who works in his community as a ceremonialist and a guide for contacting one's own spiritual center and heart.

Contact Rick Sievers at:
ricksfarm@yahoo.com

Rick's websites:
www.fieldofsevehouses.com
www.fieldofsevenhouses.blogspot.com